The Family Guide To
A Successful Life

By
Farris Patterson

The Family Guide to A Successful Life©

All rights reserved. No part of this book may be reproduced or transmitted in any form or by any means, electronic or mechanical, including photocopying, recording, or by any information storage and retrieval system, without written permission from the publisher. Please contact Burkwood Media for more information:

Burkwood Media & Consulting

P O Box 29448

Charlotte, NC 28229

Preface

Do you ever imagine or dream? How often as a child did you daydream? If you did daydream, I bet you were told to stop daydreaming. Well, I want to show you that daydreaming is not so bad after all.

In this book, I will share with you secrets that have been around for thousands of years. It is the law of attraction or the law of the subconscious mind. Now you may find many books and videos of authors, celebrities and just ordinary people who give testimonies of how the law of attraction worked for them.

I remember my first experience with the law of attraction at eight years old. My mother had given me a rubber baseball, and my youngest uncle and I would often play catch with it in our backyard. I had become very attached to this ball. However, one day, while we were playing, the ball vanished. We could not find it anywhere. I cannot begin to tell you how upset I was that day. We looked everywhere. We searched all over that backyard. I put so much thought and energy into wondering what happened to the ball. My thoughts were so in-depth that I went to bed with the vision of my baseball on my mind.

Well, that night in a dream I saw the ball was in a storm drain in our backyard. Even though we had already looked there physically, my dream revealed that the ball was just sitting there. That morning as soon as the sun started to rise, while still wearing my pajamas, I put on my shoes and went directly to that storm drain. Low and behold there was my ball. It was in the exact place that I had envisioned.

My purpose for writing this book is to help families to envision a healthier and prosperous life. Even though many can benefit from reading this book I especially want to assist families, single parents and college students. This book is not just about wealth but relationships, happiness and good health. This book is my first, and I am delighted to share with you what I have learned from authors such as Neville Goddard, Florence Scovel Shinn, and Joseph Murphy. I want to deliver a similar message differently. I've used these methods to find joy and happiness with myself, my marriage and to build a better relationship with my children. So, consider me your personal life coach.

As you read this book, I want to encourage you to meditate and dream again. And to believe that everything you desire is possible and will happen. As you meditate and dream again, you will impart to your children the same methodology and motivate them to do the same, which will lead them to success.

Dedication

I dedicate this book to my grandmother, the late Susie Patterson, who catapulted this push to greatness in me at six years old. Even then, she knew I had a special gift that would help many.

I also want to thank my wife, Lee Anne and my former spouse, Kim, for displaying peace, character, and friendship that surpasses all understanding in my life and the lives of our children.

Thirdly, I want to thank everyone whom I have had the pleasure of speaking life into and for those who just needed an ear. You are the ones who trusted me enough to grant me access into your personal lives and stories. I am forever grateful.

I also thank those who will purchase and read this book. I know this book will be a blessing to you.

"In this world there is Ego, and if there is Ego, there's always Opinions, and if there is always Opinions, there will always be Religion."

Farris Patterson

Table of Contents

Preface..i

Dedication...ii

Chapter 1 – Husband and Wife............................1

Chapter 2 – The Subconscious Mind..................13

Chapter 3 – Children..23

Chapter 4 – The Law..31

Chapter 5 – See Beyond......................................39

Chapter 6 – The Soul...49

Chapter 7 – Friends...57

Chapter 8 – Who Am I?.......................................65

Chapter 9 – Where do you live?........................73

About the Author..81

Chapter One

Husband and Wife

There are several published books, online articles, and YouTube videos discussing the application of the universal law of imagination, the law of attraction or power of the subconscious mind. Many scientists have studied the universal law and found it to be quite remarkable. Some have admitted that there is something greater in the universe. Luminaries such as Plato, Beethoven, and Charles Fillmore all understood the law of attraction.

Understand you are God's creation. Created by the one true God. Different religions use several names for God, yet when we research the deity of God, all would agree that no matter how we reference God, the deity is the same. According to Webster, Religion means, a personal set or institutionalized system of religious attitudes, beliefs, and practices. Christians today refer to God as God. In the old testament God was called El, Yahweh or Jehovah, Elohim-The Creator, Elyon-The Most High, El Shaddai-My supply, Jehovah-Rophe-My healer, Jehovah-Nissi-My victory just to name a few. These also are the deity of God.

As for Islam, God is called Allah, but there are 99 attributes of Allah such as Ar Rahman- The all Merciful, Ar Rahim-The Most Merciful, Al Malik-The King, The Sovereign, Al Quddus-

The Most Holy, just to name a few. These attributes are the deity of God.

As for the Baha'i religion, Baha is God or All-Glorious. As for the Baha'is faith, there are also many attributes of God which are the deity of God such as Allah-u-Abha –God is All Glorious, Ya Baha u'l-Abha –O Thou Glory of the Most Glorious, Baha'u'llah-The Glory of God, to name a few.

As you see, many monotheistic religions, believe the one true God is the universe and infinite in all things. The deity of God is described as gods within God and also considered as the attributes of God. The attributes are pure energy. Why? Because the kingdom of Heaven doesn't see sickness, poverty, hatred or any other negative energy. Meaning when the world presents such actions, you immediately call on the energy for which will substitute the positive for the negative. For instance, you place your faith on what you know God will provide. Even though your circumstance may show financial lack, El Shaddai, this energy in which you believe will supply what you need.

Monotheistic is the belief that God is the one true God of the universe and all things in it. My intent is not to delve too deeply into the religious aspect of each faith. My goal is to help you understand why we should focus on God and the message of love knowing God is love, peace and the One in which we can all trust. My personal belief is that God created us in his image. Now understanding Creation means to understand the creator. Throughout the new testament, Jesus talked about "the good news." The good news was that the kingdom of God was at hand. Humanity's sins had them bound in mental slavery through the law of Moses. However, the kingdom brought forth deliverance. Christians believe Jesus is the gateway to the kingdom. In other words, to trust in Jesus was to trust in God and his ways of love that the man Jesus demonstrated while on earth. Jesus possessed the fruit of the Spirit which is love, joy, peace, forbearance, kindness, goodness, faithfulness, gentleness and self-control. Religious interpretations may sometimes misinterpret the message Jesus was trying to convey to be not a message of love but as a message of condemnation. Jesus wasn't here on earth to condemn anyone but for believers to trust in him as he was one with God. He also wants everyone to know because he has risen, any who accepts him enters his Kingdom. That Kingdom is rest from any worry, doubt or any negative thought. Those who believe will be free from the bondage of the law of Moses. Jesus did not come to condemn the law that was given to Moses by the All Mighty but to fulfill the law and disband condemnation with love and forgiveness. The problem is when we hear the word Bible, we think religion. The Bible has a plethora of rules by which one should live. I want to help you understand that God is love. Jesus' message was love. Let us realize that our love is tested daily in our relationships, but overcoming these obstacles is evident whether or not we possess unconditional love. This unconditional love God displays for us includes joy, peace, forbearance, kindness, goodness, faithfulness, gentleness and self-control. Measure your love for your spouse by these standards regardless of the negatives that may be in your present relationship. Before you effectively walk in and experience the fruit of the spirit, you must first practice forgiveness. Your mindset should change from the things that are not pure of God. As you embrace this mindset, you begin to understand that through your possession of the power of God, you alone possess what you need to heal yourself and others. Through your healing, you can be a blessing, speak life into others, yourself, enhance your marriage, and bring peace in your home. The good news preached by Jesus was that of repentance. Repentance means you must shift from negative thoughts and actions. The question may arise, where is this kingdom? This kingdom resides in your subconscious. When you put your trust in God and start to visualize what you ask in faith, you will receive. Living in the kingdom is dwelling in peace with your mind and knowing you don't stress, worry or doubt the God in you and the Spirit of God that directs your thoughts.

My first area to address towards a successful journey begins in your home. The initial step is to understand your spouse. To understand someone else is to look for the good in them and not the bad. A person shouldn't be so quick to judge the one he or she loves. As you are understanding and loving your spouse, remember to take the time to reflect on yourself. What are some things you see about yourself that need to change to make you a better you? I would say practice the fruit of the spirit as I mentioned earlier. Open your heart and mind by meditating before you go to bed on the positive qualities your spouse possesses. When you both met, there was a shared deep-down happiness. You found yourself dreaming of just being together. There was no judgment or negative thoughts about each other. If there were negative vibes, I wouldn't think you would want to continue dating let alone marry this person. Ask yourself, what changed? Ask yourself, did you stop dreaming? Did you stop seeing your wife/ husband as the most beautiful person in the world? If you aren't sure, then take a moment to reflect on these questions. Your responses will help you to determine what you may be missing in your relationship.

- Do you tell your spouse you love her or him constantly without a second thought?

- When you have disagreements are you as careful not to hurt the others feeling as when you first fell in love?

If you find yourself out of sync when it comes to love, this could be your energies aren't in alignment with the universe. Remember God is the universe. God is energy, and God is love. You both are energy, and you both are love. If the love fades, then your alignment is off. Children start acting out with bad behavior for this very reason. They are around negativity at school daily because young people can be mean. The children who are on social media can be cruel as well. The daily encounters with negativity adds to the negative energy a child or children will feel at home. The child will begin to feel as if he or she is not loved. These feelings manifest due to the lack of love witnessed and experienced daily.

Remember what you put out is what comes back. Follow these simple steps:

1. Keep everything positive about your spouse. Regardless of the struggle, shift it into a positive experience. Don't constantly remind them of what they do but always be

thankful for the little things. If your spouse doesn't engage in anything such as taking out the trash or picking up after themselves, then see them doing what you ask before you ask. Create a positive energy so what you see will start to manifest. And most of all be patient if what you vision doesn't happen overnight.

2. See your spouse as the love of your life, and there is no other person with whom you would like to share life. Visualize you and your spouse on a romantic getaway. Have "date night" with the same energy you had when you first started dating.

3. Make sure your spouse feels like he or she is the luckiest person on earth because you were chosen to be in their life. This thought process will create a positive energy in your house. Your child will also feel the overwhelming sense of love in the home.

4. At night before you go to bed, meditate for about fifteen to twenty minutes, meditate on things you want to happen in your marriage and your spouse. Visualize those things as though they are happening now. Don't spend time talking about or focusing on the negative things that may have happened today or what you think may happen tomorrow. Once you have created a positive aura within your mind, the same energy will represent itself in your future.

5. Always be thankful for your family, job and the people around you. Realize everyone in your circle of space is there for a reason. Once you gravitate to a high space of consciousness, you will see a shift in your life. People who are

not meant to be in your life will either move or be moved by you. You may get promoted or move to a better place in life by way of another job or becoming an entrepreneur.

These steps will change the way you think and will have a tremendous impact on your road to a successful life. Please understand, I am never opposed to family counseling. Family counseling may serve as a tool to help you and your spouse understand things and perspectives you may not be able to get each other to see. Communication is the key to any successful marriage. Without communication in a marriage, the two will not be able to come into agreement. Once you have made that conscious decision of what your spouse doesn't do, it transcends to your subconscious mind. Now here we are discussing the subconscious mind again. Remember you are a creator so if you see your spouse behaving in a manner then maybe you should ask yourself, "Did I create this?" When I speak on how I see him or her act, and I say," He or she will never change," did I do this? My suggestion is you go to counseling with an open mind. View only the positive in every conversation and try not to feel offended by your spouse's feelings towards your actions. Let the fruit of the spirit and the God that dwells in you take over. You will see a tremendous burden lifted from your shoulders.

No marriage is perfect unless you make it perfect. You and your spouse are fallible beings and will make mistakes. You or your spouse will have bad days. Sometimes you may find yourself lashing out at the other or the kids. First, don't take it personal. Instead, find ways to comfort your spouse. As you comfort him or her, take the time to visualize them smiling peacefully and just enjoying your presence. The atmosphere is calm as a sense of love and peace flows in you and around you. Remember this book is about the law of attraction which is visualization. If your spouse doesn't show signs of calming down, then let him or her have some peaceful time alone to collect their thoughts as you continue to visualize him or her smiling and laughing.

If you are a pessimistic person, you will attract only the negative aspects of your relationship. If you only visualize the negative, you should never expect to have a positive outcome. Pessimists fail to realize they are painting a grim picture of their life.

To make the law of attraction serve as a benefit in your life, you would want to be optimistic about everything. Being an optimist means you will look at every situation with hope. No matter what is in front of you, know you can visualize and speak a brighter outcome right then and there. Jesus once said, "Your faith has healed you." In other words, you thought if you got near me, saw me or touched me, healing would come to you. Through our continuous faith in what we speak and what we know, the God in us can perform the same miracles as Jesus. Faith in yourself, your vision and your words activates the law of attraction. The activation still holds true when you unconsciously think negatively. You want to be aware of your thoughts. Being conscious of your thoughts trains you to think positive which produce outcomes.

You may feel the two of you can't afford a getaway. But ask yourself, how many times have you told yourself you can't afford a getaway? Have you ever told yourself you and your spouse could go on a getaway? The law of attraction doesn't deal in the future but deals in the present. Let me give some steps that will help you and your spouse to plan a fantastic vacation.

1. You should discuss a spot you would like to go. Research prices and plan. Don't look at the cost and say, "We could never afford that."

2. Post pictures on the wall or your computer and look at them every day. The law of visualization is in effect here.

3. Put away a few dollars but don't be concerned about the amount. Stay in the now.

4. Tell yourself and friends you are going on a fantastic getaway soon.

5. Smile and enjoy the pictures as though you are there.

6. Meditate on the trip before you go to bed, imagining you and your spouse enjoying all the amenities your getaway should offer.

7. Once the vision becomes a part of you, don't get frustrated but understand the law of the universe will attract this vision, and you will see money come from nowhere.

I was offered a job in California while living in Georgia. I put in my two weeks' notice in preparation of moving to California. I had wanted to relocate to California for some time. I visualized the house and community in which my family and I would live. I even visualized the type of school my kids would attend. Well, the job offer didn't come to fruition. For a moment, I admit I was stuck. However, I continued the move. Three days later, I landed a great job. I didn't have moving expenses, but I needed to get my vehicle from Georgia to California. I bought two plane tickets from California to Atlanta to get my car and belongings from a relative's house. My wife and I drove back with $300.00 in our account. As we were driving through Mississippi, my car's suspension blew. We had to get a hotel for a night and pay for repairs. We found an inexpensive hotel for $60, and due to the generosity of a kind mechanic, the cost of repairs was about $55. Now we are left with $185. We now must go 4,000 miles on $185. Not once did we question how were we going to make it. We had already arrived in our mind that God had made a way. When we arrived outside of Dallas, I was going to buy a GPS device from Walmart so I wouldn't get lost when suddenly I heard a voice say, *"check your account."* When I checked my bank account, there was a deposit of $3,500.00 dollars. I didn't know where it came from and I didn't use any of the money because we made it on the $185. I waited for a month, and the bank didn't indicate any error on their end, but there was indeed an anonymous deposit made in my account. While the bank did not know the source, I knew the source was God. The vision of living in California was already done by faith and belief - not based on the presented circumstances.

Chapter Two

The Subconscious Mind

This chapter describes the wonders of the subconscious mind. The subconscious mind does not negotiate what you believe. It merely creates what you believe. If you see yourself never having money, you will always struggle financially. If you feel you will never succeed in life, you will always fall beneath your potential. The conscious mind reasons with doubt and fear because the world we live in always presents fear or doubt. When you hear your children repeat what they can't do, what you have regularly told them they could not do or any negativity, is because they only reproduce the seeds planted in them. Have you ever wondered how hypnosis works? It's the same principal. The only difference is someone else is choosing to put in your subconscious mind what they want to manifest. Other laws work alongside the law of the subconscious mind; the law of attraction, the law of suggestion, the law of cause and effect just to name a few. You will see many of these laws rear the same results, but with different names.

The law of attraction is the continuous thoughts you have that are to the point of belief is what you attract. This law coincides with the subconscious mind.

The law of suggestion is what hypnotists use. When a hypnotist suggests that you are something other than yourself or perhaps suggest certain things about your five senses, the subconscious mind will yield to these suggestions.

The law of cause and effect is also known as karma. In the Bible Galatians 6:7 reads, "Be not deceived; God is not mocked: for whatsoever a man soweth, that shall he also reap." The law of cause and effect is the same as sowing seeds of good thoughts, except it goes a little deeper. This law deals with action as well as thought. Let's say you have a repeated thought in your mind that you chose not to let people out when entering onto the street with their vehicle. Instead, you prohibit their entrance without a thought. Now, you fail to realize you have a negative seed that will come back to you. You are leaving the grocery store, and you are in a rush to get home. Traffic is heavy, and no one wants to let you cut into the flow of traffic. You find yourself waiting 12 to 15 minutes before traffic lightens up and you are frustrated. Well, remember you only get what you put out. As the old saying goes, *"karma is a bitch."*

Dr. Wayne Dyer called the law of attraction the power of intention. He stated that he never liked laws or rules. His belief was you attract what you are. You may see books or audios by authors who speak of "I am." In Exodus 3:1-15 Moses spoke to a burning bush which was God. God had commanded that he speak to the Israelites concerning their captivity by the Egyptians. He was preparing the Elders and leaders to speak to Pharaoh. Moses asked, "God who shall I say sent me?" "God said tell them I am sent you." With "I am" being a powerful statement, Dr. Dyer believed when you are in the "I am" state of mind, that is what you become. You do this by first saying and believing in yourself. Speak to yourself and say, "I am love, I am peace, I am joy." Now, this principle doesn't change its alignment with the other laws as they all harvest a thought of love, peace, and happiness. But Dr. Dyer didn't think the focused attraction should be material things. I agree if we only see those things, we are out of alignment with God. It is important to understand the material things will naturally come if you are about being on the correct path which is your purpose on this earth. In Matthew 19:16-22 Jesus is speaking to this rich man about giving up his possessions. Now the man seems to want to be perfect on earth as he carefully obeys the ten commandments passed down from Moses. Jesus understood this but asked if he would be willing to give up his possessions to the poor. He then would have treasures in heaven. The man could not part with his possessions. The treasures in heaven undoubtedly are in the subconscious mind. We need to understand that anyone can obtain anything on this earth. The determination is, who we put our trust in to get them. Proverbs 3:5-6 reads, "Trust in the Lord with all of your heart and lean not on your own understanding; in all your ways submit to him, and he will make your paths straight." I know I said that the God in you allows you to accomplish all things, but you must be willing to let God direct you and not venture out in your own thought or strength. Enter God's rest from trying so hard, and He will direct your path to perfect works. Things you do for others will not only bring you joy, but you will see an abundance.

As we see, many of the spiritual laws of this universe influence how we think, feel or act. Our subconscious mind processes the conscious mind to reach a decision on what we are to believe and what our conscious mind is suggesting. Once you have made a conscious decision whether good or bad, this is how the subconscious lives. You are a creator in God's image which also means you have the ability to create. You were designed to speak those things that are not as though they are, Romans 4:17. There are millions of people in the world who speak negative and positive. Your mind has free will to pull down in your imagination whatever you chose to hear and believe. When consciousness struggles with good and bad thoughts, your mind becomes a battlefield as Author Joyce Meyers puts it. Once you make up your mind of what thought you choose; you are sure to see the outcome of that thought. In Joshua 24:15, the Israelites died in the desert because of a hardened heart, a heart of unbelief, a lack of vision. A lack of trust. The next generation did believe, did trust God, trusted their vision and with vision did possess the land God promised. The faith exhibited was figurative to show that trusting in God (The Universe and all its glory) will give you a promise that will be given and will be forever. Now not to confuse you when I said earlier the subconscious mind doesn't know good or bad. Let's look at this story of the Israelites. God only wants the best for us, so the voice of God spoke. God's voice represents positive thoughts. At times, you will hear a positive thought or intuition to do something. When you trust that thought and because you feel very strongly about it - you act on it. The result mirrors what was in your subconscious mind. The same occurs with negative thoughts. Negative thoughts can come out of anger which will be a vindictive thought. Once you act on that thought, you may feel satisfied for a moment, but once thought about, you realize it wasn't worth it, and the outcome wasn't that gratifying. Nevertheless, the outcome was exactly how you pictured. When negative thoughts come, I believe there is a split second to come to a conscious decision that this idea is not good. There is a God conscious within that decides whether something is good or bad.

Denying yourself the ability to succeed is denying the God within you merely stop believing He loves you because you stop loving yourself. Whenever something in your subconscious mind tells you, you can't do something; you are telling God what He promised you and all humanity is a lie. Your mind is no longer at rest; therefore, you begin worrying and stressing about your problems. Everything you will do from this point will be a reaction from fear. For example, in one of Jesus' parables, he spoke about the kingdom of God, Matthew 13:1. This parable of the sower describes how seeds fell upon different soils. The "soil" or "ground" is the subconscious mind. The "seed" is what you believe consciously or unconsciously. The seeds are thought produced creativity using the law of attraction. Remember when you constantly keep these thoughts of fear, failure or doubt, you are planting a seed. Trust me; this is the harvest you will reap. The downside is the harvest produced will be a harvest of weeds. Who in their life has ever seen a beautiful weed? The results are opposite when you sow a seed of good thoughts? With faith, no matter the circumstance, you will reap a beautiful garden. Reaping the harvest of a beautiful garden, is fertile ground, good ground. Hard ground will represent doubt or unbelief, and nothing grows other than weeds. When you have negative thoughts in your subconscious mind, the law of attraction will attract weeds in your life. To sum it up, the law of attraction is what you put in your subconscious mind. Whether it is faith or fear, good or bad, what you plant is what will produce.

The world fails to realize every day our subconscious mind is working on our behalf. Take your organs, for example, your heart, lungs, kidneys function normally without you negotiating with the conscious mind whether they should work or not. Take note; I did not say, if you consciously start to put fear into your subconscious mind that your heart is weak or your kidneys may be failing they may just do as you suggest. The particular law in action here is the law of suggestion. The law of suggestion works along with the subconscious mind. For instance, if you suggest you are sick and you need to go to a doctor. (Now I will tell anyone if you feel you need a checkup then do so.) If the doctor runs tests and a week later gives you tests result which could be positive for some sickness, immediately you would go into a panic, and you start to tell yourself you knew something was going on. You are suggesting you have that sickness. What happens if you later find out the results were a mistake? How would your subconscious mind process the information? Initially, you feel a certain way. Maybe you are having sharp chest pains. In that case, you need to seek medical attention. However, in personal instances, I choose to take the approach of meditating and relaxing, thus allowing the God in me to speak to my organs that He created and maintained functionality without my knowledge. I then speak to my situation as in the case, "I am relaxed, and the pains will subside." Most of the time, we are quick to accept the negative from others before we accept the positive in ourselves. If you are a hypochondriac, you will have to purge yourself of all the negatives embedded in the subconscious mind. Negative images of your health will only lead you to stress and allow the subconscious mind to control your moods or well-being on a negative plain.

I have shared with many of my coaching clients, when you carry a fear or mistrust you must realize it is a choice. For a thought scenario, I ask people if they think about the yellow line in the middle of the road when they are driving? Most say they don't give it a thought. I inform them their subconscious mind has put them at ease, so they don't have a grim picture of a car swerving out of control or just barely crossing the line and hitting them. Now, this could change for some if this was to happen. From this point, the only image ingrained in the subconscious is the continuous image of a car crossing the line. Because of the incident, fear settles in. It is not to say they will attract this again but the thought could have once come that they witnessed this and the picture painted until the universe presented the very act. Again, we must be quick to release negative thoughts immediately.

The same goes for a chair you may sit in every day. Your subconscious mind doesn't negotiate with your conscious mind whether you should sit in a chair or not. Safety is determined by what if any potential danger is present and your conscious mind will debate if it is safe to sit in the chair. Once you make up your conscious mind, it paints a picture of you sitting in that chair and you will speak into existence "I feel this is safe." It is likely you were correct in your observation. Everything created on earth began with a thought. Just as God's creation, everything was spoken into existence. When a man thinks of a thing he feels excited. He starts to visualize and from that visualization, an energy is created that will drive him to mold his vision. Sometimes there can be restraints such as money. Depending on the level of positive thought and belief, God will provide what is needed. All a person must do is let the universe take over. Let God make the provision, and not try to figure out how it comes to pass. I know for sure this doesn't happen when a person is visualizing something negative that will cause harm. What God has for us is everlasting. But we must continue with the same positive thoughts and good vibrations. Never let go of the good God has placed in you. Continue to grow by giving and stay focused on what's above and not the material things on this earth. Philippians 4:4-8, "Rejoice in the Lord always; again I will say, rejoice. Let your reasonableness be known to everyone. The Lord is at hand; do not be anxious about anything, but in everything by prayer and supplication with thanksgiving let your requests be made known to God. And the peace of God, which surpasses all understanding, will guard your hearts and your minds in Christ Jesus. Finally, brothers, whatever is true, whatever is honorable, whatever is just, whatever is pure, whatever is lovely, whatever is commendable, if there is any excellence, if there is anything worthy of praise, think about these things." In other words, be excited about what you vision. At the appointed time, you will receive all you ask; therefore, there is no need to become anxious. Being anxious is a way of telling the universe you are not trusting what you want will be manifested. God doesn't work by time because the universe is timeless. During Jesus' ministry, He demonstrated the concept of time as parallel to when people waited for him to provide a miracle. When He allowed days to pass before the evidence of the miracle, He proved to man that time didn't matter. Show God your love is patient and you are willing to wait for the manifestation of what he has given you.

Chapter Three

Children

Your children are precious, and they are truly a gift from God. Sometimes we get so involved in our day to day life that we forget the gift. A child coming into this world is an innocent lost little human who is trusting only in this large person. The same large person with whom they wish to share a connection. The person with the child may not be the biological parent but a guardian or one who has adopted. As a child grows and matures, they start to take on the spirit of the one who is raising him or her. Between the ages of two and five years old it is said to be a crucial learning bracket for a child. At this age, they will pick up behavior traits from the parents or guardian. These tender years are the time you want to plant positive seeds in your child.

Children have always had a God given discernment. Due to their innocent nature; a child is pure, non-judgmental and loving. Matthew 18:3 describes their innocence. Jesus said, "I say to you, unless you turn and become like children, you will not enter the kingdom of heaven." The kingdom of heaven is to enter into God's rest from any worry, judgment or convictions, but as a child grows, parents, television, peers, and social media influences their maturity. These influencing factors can be negative or positive, depending on what their subconscious mind starts to accept. As parents, we want to be sure we only speak positive to our children. Be mindful to keep any arguments or differences away from them. Don't allow them to see or hear the discord. When children encounter disagreements, they immediately assume their parents don't love each other. The child takes these emotions and concludes they may be the problem thus meaning he or she isn't loved. The feeling of not being loved could motivate changes in the child's behavior. These changes could very well affect them academically by impeding their concentration in school and with their overall focus.

Love your child and take the time to see your child doing great things. Discuss with your child the positive vision you see for his or her life. Plant a seed of love and hope that your child will cherish. Love and positive thinking will overshadow anything a child faces from peers in school or even through social media. He or she will automatically shun themselves from any negativity because the negative doesn't reflect the love felt in their home and from the parent(s). Daily Prayer and meditation will not only cleanse your soul of all negative vibrations but will bring about a positive effect which leads to a successful life for your child.

Let's look closely at the pre-teen years. The preteen years are the ages of 11 and 12. The children in this age group tend to take on an identity. Peer pressure becomes more of an issue during these years as they become more influenced by what their peers may think or feel about them. As parents, we make attempts to understand what they may be experiencing, and we should always assure them they are loved, and they are perfect in our eyes. In some cases, the positive reinforcement doesn't carry over well. Therefore, a battle ensues. Our next area of discussion is the battle parents face with reassuring their child.

As I have mentioned in the earlier chapter, the subconscious mind develops what we see or believe. Because of the innocence of children, they will have a greater manifestation of their belief because once convinced; children tend to lock on without judgment or doubt. How many times have you seen or heard of a child speaking of how disappointed they were if a parent told them they would do something repeatedly but it didn't happen? I have seen children living with one parent (mainly the mother) and the father promised to spend time with the child, but is either late or never shows. The mother becomes angry, and her frustration is evident. She begins to speak negative things to the child about the father. After a while, the child's subconscious mind starts to paint a negative image of how they see their father based on the seeds the mother planted through her frustration. If the father gets his act together, the child only sees the negative picture. No matter how much time the father spends with the child or how many gifts he buys, the child's impression of his or her father is ingrained and difficult to change. This example is not to say the father will always deal with distance and negativity towards him. Mothers may also experience the same as the child may be with the father full time.

All broken relationships can be mended because love conquers all. God is love, and everything about God is love. To love yourself is to love God. To love your child is to love God. If you want love in return, we must present love. A father may feel as though "my son or daughter wants nothing to do with me." Well if that's how you feel then that is the outcome you will get. Once you understand positive always overpowers negative, you will understand how speaking positively about your relationship with your children results in a change in how they view you. You will have to be patient as not all things happen suddenly. Trust in God who dwells in you and lean not to your own understanding in the matter. Each day you should wake up joyous as you continue with the internal vision of you and your child enjoying the day laughing together. Your vision is in the now and not the future. Never say, "I hope one day" as the universe only deals with the present. The present we live in speaks of I am. Declare this, "I am a happy father or mother." "My child" (say the child's name ") is precious and wonderful, and I am glad I have him or her in my life. We have an excellent relationship not based on material things, but strictly on the love God has given us through the universe which allows all good things to manifest. I am love. I am peace. Therefore, I only attract peace, and I only attract love." Make this declaration every day even if you don't see any manifestation of what you speak. Trust God that you will see a change.

Understand your child doesn't understand life as you do. Your child hasn't experienced much living even though you may hear he or she speak as though they are older than you. It is ego. Everyone has an ego, and ego normally drives people to behave the way they do. God doesn't deal with ego. Ego is not a humbling spirit. When children allow their ego to take over, the parent must not allow their ego to compete with the children's. Ego in this present time will always cause division or disagreements to turn into arguments and unforgiveness. If you want to tame the ego, you must align yourself with the universe. God is the universe and everything in it. Humble yourself before God. Humble doesn't mean you are a weak person, but to humble yourself means you are putting your trust in infinite wisdom. You are putting your trust in the almighty God. You didn't create the universe nor did you create anything in it. God knows for He is infinite wisdom. Trusting in God will certainly tame your ego. Egotistical people often struggle with respect from others. They always feel things should go their way. Now there is nothing wrong with wanting things to go your way but if you force this before it's time it will not be from God but your own egotistical spirit. Put your trust in God, and in your subconscious mind that the vision you will see is pure and happy. With a joyful spirit, your ego has no control, but all you ask will be given. Your path will be directed to the correct path to bring about whatever you shall ask.

When you see your child's ego start to run or control their thoughts or ways, just smile and never argue with the ego. Ephesians 6:12, "For we wrestle not against flesh and blood, but against principalities, against powers, against the rulers of the darkness of this world, against spiritual wickedness in high places." This scripture explains how we battle with ego and not the person. The spiritual wickedness is the negative the ego embraces. Let God deal with the ego in your child. Trust your child to understand and allow life to take over. Parents are afraid of allowing their child to experience life teaching ordeals. We must always rely on the intelligence of God when an experience happens that it's not necessarily negative but grounding. Remember grounding means to humble. When your child becomes grounded, they can experience an open mind to receive positive words to allow a fulfilled manifestation.

Proverbs 18:21, "Life and death is in the tongue." The tongue can bring death or life; those who love to talk will reap the consequences. A critical time for your child is when the ego is open to receive all negative. The words you speak plant seeds in the subconscious mind. The words will seem convincing to your child because they are at a sponge absorbent age. I think this is funny because they can like school and suddenly, they hate school. Who is around them that hates school? Who is influencing their mind? You should ask yourself and ask your child. Life and death don't solely mean your physical body. God is not concerned about a body which will return to the earth. God is concerned about your soul or the inner being. It is damaging for a child to hear contradicting or wrong words such as, "You are so stupid, or you are lazy or if you choose to fail it's fine with me." I remember I would call my oldest lazy because of my frustration with his actions, but unbeknownst to me, I was shaping his ego. Once I understood my actions, I asked God and my oldest son for forgiveness. I spoke positive things to the universe which I started to see manifest in his life. Now as a young adult he is energetic and willing to work hard. Never say it's too late when it comes to your child. It is never too late. For God doesn't live by man's time. Remember, time doesn't exist in the universe. I often think about the old hymn which refers to God as an "on time God." We don't have the power to dictate time. What we speak through faith and not fear or negative negates all time.

Speak in a manner the ego will be molded and shaped in with confidence. Again, there will be challenges in your child's life. Without challenges, your child will never mature to deal with adversity. This guide for your child to succeed in life requires you the parent be very attentive and aware as to what you speak, as well as the vibration you give out. Every day will not be a rosy day, and I'm not implying it will be. But you have the power to realign yourself each day to achieve a successful life. Let God Be God in molding your child's life. Meditate on what God has for your child each day. Speak positive affirmations to yourself such as, "I am a great parent, and the holy spirit will guide me the direct way I should go in dealing with my child." The Holy Spirit is the Spirit of God. John 14:26, "But the Advocate, the Holy Spirit, whom the Father will send in my name, will teach you all things and will remind you of everything I have said to you." When you meditate, you learn to breath; breathing brings on a calmness. The breath we breathe is God's breath. Man didn't create the oxygen you are breathing. Every living thing needs this breath. It is God who breathes breath into man. You will find by relaxing and breathing calmly, allows answers to fill your spirit. You would be amazed how your child will connect with your spirit.

I am convinced that in today's time, some doctors look for modern medicine to "cure" our kids. Society will place a name or title to every activity that doesn't fit society. After this medicine will follow. Say you are driving a top of the line, finely tuned vehicle and a mechanic tells you to use an additive to make your car run better. Now you realize the car was built and running fine without the additive. This additive represents the pills doctors want to give your child to calm them down because he or she feels this will change the chemicals in the brain. So, the additive can't adjust the computer (the brain). The automobile manufacturer should have a positive solution for your car; such as God has an answer for your child. Pray and believe is the best antidote I can give you. When you pray, know you will receive.

To summarize this chapter: We addressed that your child is a gift from God and a joy to parent. Always stay positive about your child and around your child. If you make a promise to your child, then keep it. Don't try, just do. Vision what you want to do with your child and know it is possible and is already done. What we do is what we first see. Then you can promise. A promise is a spoken agreement, but also a vision with faith acts on it. There is a certainty when it comes to promises. God promised us an everlasting life if we believe. Many people have chosen to trust these words come to know everything they received is from God and not by their own doing. Mold your child's ego with positive thoughts and practice patience when change isn't immediately seen. Proverbs 22:6, "Train up a child in the way he should go; even when he is old he will not depart from it." I can personally attest to this scripture. When I became a grown man, I got in some trouble, but what brought me to understand I was going in the wrong direction was the teaching my grandmother instilled in my mind. Don't worry if you don't see a sudden change in your child. Just understand when the season comes for a change, for sure a change will come.

Chapter Four

The Law

According to Webster's dictionary, there are several different meanings of the term "law." From my understanding and interpretation, a law is a rule established for the mind or body to be governed and grounded to maintain a positive outcome. For instance, police are put in place to ensure the public is grounded and abides by the laws in place. In doing so, it is regularly maintaining law and order which is a positive outcome. For each electrical component to work properly and to get a positive result, a ground must be available. Another example is the electrical components in your car and your home. Humans attract energy because we are an energy source and a magnet. If we are grounded, then we have a better chance of withstanding a lightning strike. These examples show you how being grounded is one of the attributes of the law which is cause and effect. All laws whether physical or universal have a cause and effect. Take for instance the law of cause and effect is the same as the law of reaping and sowing. This law also coincides with the law of compensation. This law dictates we indeed must inherit the abundance of wealth but like many laws falls under faith. In James 1-15, the Bible speaks of the testing of our faith. When we face trials, we won't be lacking what is needed to get through our trial but yet remain grounded in God.

When you have a vision, you must stay grounded in your belief of that vision. Any hint of doubting hinders the positive outcome. You have lost the grounded thought and no longer energetic about what you saw or believed. Bear in mind being grounded keeps us in a present state. You will always say "I am." We should fall under the law of energy because we are energy. Albert Einstein said, "Everything is energy, and that's all there is to it." Allow your energy to match the frequency of the reality you want, and you cannot help but obtain that reality. It can be no other way. This is not philosophy. This is physics. Einstein also quoted, "Matter is energy...Energy is light..." We are all Light Beings. Now as you see I always use the bible as a reference since the Bible is God inspired words. As aforementioned, the Bible is not a religious reference. A bible is a tool filled with God inspired words meant to help us understand what we speak or believe is what we create. Let's look at a few parables Jesus spoke while performing the sermon on the mount. In Matthew 5:3 Jesus says, "Blessed are the poor in spirit for theirs is the kingdom of God." The word blessed means "happy." The biggest part of understanding the word happy is knowing the universe is God and God is about joy, peace, and righteousness. The law of attraction itself doesn't know good or bad, but this law is God Consciousness. When God made man in his image, it meant man is also a creator. You can create bad with bad thoughts. The ability to create good manifests itself when you possess the desire to maintain a state of happiness regardless of unfavorable circumstances. No matter what the circumstance may reflect at the moment, you are happy the positive picture you so desire will manifest. The positive thoughts and overall outlook will shift your circumstance from negative to positive. You cannot create positive outcomes from negative thoughts. When you attempt to do so, it only results in excuses as to why your life never produces a greater desire. In Matthew 5:3 Jesus refers to the poor in spirit. Poor in spirit is a person who hasn't made material possessions as a way of happiness.

God wants us to be prosperous and have all we desire. However, what often happens is a man's spirit or ego becomes more focused on the material wealth that is possessed and not the good intent of the world. Therefore, without knowing, he or she will become self- centered, arrogant, lover of themselves and no one else will particularly matter. Those who are humbled and grounded will not think of their outward situation or the lack of material things but are now more content with the things of God, and the universe has presented to them. A poor man in his humbled state opens his mind to receive Gods instructions and directions. Therefore, he becomes cheerful, patient, content. His positive attitude will alleviate all stress, and he will attract good health, prosperity and a desire to do his life purpose. "For his is the kingdom of God" explains he has inherited the kingdom of God because the kingdom of God is righteousness, peace, and joy in the holy spirit...the spirit of God. Let's look at another parable. Jesus mentioned in Matthew 5:14-16, "You are the light of the world." As you go on to read the verses, you will understand to be a light means you must be energized by some fuel. Once you realize your happiness creates a positive fuel (motivation), it will not only provide light for others, but light for yourself and everyone will see this light. This law is not complicated or meant to bind you into ritualistic thinking. The law of attraction is a way of living and an explanation of how God's intended purpose for you is to be happy.

Motion pictures such as "Lucy" and the comedy "Bruce Almighty," show us we can create, be intuitive and have the ability to be all knowing. For God did create us in his image. The movie Lucy is about an American girl who lives in Taiwan. Her boyfriend tricked her into working as a drug mule. She thought she was delivering a simple package. The drugs are sewn into her abdomen but rupture before she arrives for the removal. The drug is CHP4 is a fictional drug, but for the sake of the movie, the writer says it's a chemical compound women produce in 6 weeks of pregnancy. Many of the scenes in the movie become a little farfetched, however, what we view as supernatural is not considered natural in God's view. The supernatural refers to that which bypasses what one's eyes can believe. I love the scene in the movie Bruce Almighty when Bruce; played by Jim Carrey, ask God; played by Morgan Freeman, to prove he is God by guessing how many fingers does is he holding behind his back. "God" answers 7 and when Bruce removes his hand from behind his back to reveal how many fingers he is holding up, it's seven just as God said. I give these examples because even Hollywood understands the all-knowing God gave us the power to speak anything in existence just as He does. I mentioned earlier that we as humans tend to think every miracle is unexplainable. Jesus preached the power of faith and the holy spirit is what dwells within us. If we practice this faith on a regular basis it will not be considered supernatural. When Peter walks on water in Matthew 14:22-33 his subconscious mind allowed him to go above what we consider unnatural yet shows when fear overcomes faith our subconscious mind takes on a new identity. Many people think the Bible is this fictional book of stories. On the contrary, I see the bible stories as figurative of what the mind does and doesn't do according to the law. To walk on water defies the law of gravity. It is very easy to denounce the power of the universe and all that is in it when you don't believe. I see comments on YouTube by readers that suggest the power of the subconscious mind is a hoax, witchcraft and so forth and so on. If we understand what Jesus meant in John 14:20, when he said, "When I am raised to life again, you will know that I am in my Father, and you are in me, and I am in you." The real indication shows we have this power with faith to create. When we read Genesis 1:27 we see and understand the Law as God intended. God created mankind in his own image. The Bible goes on to say He created them both male and female. As we read we understand God rested after the creation of man and woman. Genesis 2:5 reads "neither wild plants nor grains were growing on the earth. For the LORD God had not yet sent rain to water the earth, and there were no people to cultivate the soil." As you continue to read the remaining of Genesis, you will see the manifestation of his spoken word came to earth. Imitating God is to understand the law requires us to come to a rest with God from all work. In other words, stop trying to do what you ask God to do for you. To enter into Gods rest is to enter into his trust. God's spirit is in you and what you think or speak will be created. Therefore, it is so important to have a positive and pure thought. When people debate on the law of attraction, they don't realize this law is being used every day as people will attract the things they don't want. Also in effect, daily is the law of sowing and reaping, as they continue speaking what they can't afford or what is too much and the harvest lack or shortage in their life.

In God is everything as he created us to be everything so let us remember the subconscious mind doesn't know good or bad. Our universe has many laws, and we may tend to think of them as science. If that is your opinion then so be it. But scientists have come to understand this law supersedes much of their understanding of any law. Due to the evidence of so-called miracles being recorded all over the world.

There is a story about a man who was said to be a very healthy strong young man but seemed to be a hypochondriac. One day during the summer a train crew was informed they could leave early. They locked the train car not knowing the young man was in there. Now this train car was a refrigerator boxcar but understand this car didn't work. He banged and shouted, but no one heard him. The next morning the crew opened the doors and found him dead. He used a knife to carve the following on a piece of wood on the floor, "It's so cold my body is getting numb. If only I could just go to sleep. These may be my last words." Later the autopsy revealed the physical signs of hyperthermia killed him. How could this happen when the train car temperature dropped no lower than 66 degrees? This example is evidence of how our mind can change our state of being. In Matthew 9:18 Jesus was approached by one of the synagogue leaders to tell him his daughter just died. Jesus' intent was to attend to this man's matter right away, but a woman who had been bleeding for twelve years stopped him. The synagogue leader was in a hurry for Jesus to tend to his daughter and now Jesus has stopped to ask who touched him. Doubt has probably entered the leader's mind as he is too late to heal her or bring her alive. Jesus commanded the crowd to go away. His next comment was "she is not dead but asleep." When Jesus dismissed the crowd, he then commanded the girl to wake up." When we have faith in what we know, we can change circumstance from negative to positive. One distinct action was the need for Jesus to remove the doubtful. Peter began to sink because he was in the presence of doubters. Although they spent much time with Jesus and had seen many wonders and miracles they still did not believe. You will have critics because they haven't seen or recognized a move of God. Matthew 7:2 reads "Not everyone who says to me, 'Lord, Lord,' will enter the kingdom of heaven, but only the one who does the will of my Father who is in heaven. 22 Many will say to me on that day, 'Lord, Lord, did we not prophesy in your name and in your name, drive out demons and in your name, perform many miracles?' 23 Then I will tell them plainly, 'I never knew you. Away from me, you evildoers!" When you deny the powers of God, you deny God. The God who dwells in you is careful not to judge others without understanding them and with everyone we should see understanding with love. Jesus considered these people evil doers because they didn't practice the one true law, the law of love. God is love, and God is law. God is the universe therefore when we enter the kingdom of God we simply rest from creating our own path. Understand a creator means you create but the Spirit of God directs. With love, we come to understand people and nature without negative judgment. For if a man learns he can be healed or can heal others by meditation and prayer; using the subconscious mind shouldn't be hindered by anyone's negative belief. Why would one criticize a person of thinking of doing good to himself and his fellow brethren? This law which is the mind of God and his thinking is what God established long before creation. If you are trusting in the universal law, you won't be in bondage as you live in this world. Consider this universal law as one that isn't forced because God is freewill. Always remember you have a choice but what I'm telling you is this choice of surrendering the will to God will without a doubt lead you to a successful outcome.

Chapter Five

See Beyond

As you look at life ask yourself, who told you you need to work to pay your bills? Who told you if you don't work you will not have anything? Did you think what you do now is what you learned at a very young age? I remember after high school telling myself it was best I go into the Army because I couldn't do anything else. I honestly felt this way about myself. Once discharged from the army I told myself I didn't want to go to school and I could only do physical labor jobs to get by. I tried college a few years after leaving the military. It was an epic fail. It was a fail because I could not see myself graduating. It wasn't until I told myself I desired an office job and would make good money doing it that I started to visualize myself sitting in an office. Just sitting in an office left little to the imagination, so I imagined myself as a CADD (Computer Automated Drafting Designer). The fact that I had no formal education in this field didn't stop me from considering myself as a CADD operator. I struggled with the law of attraction for years because even though I believed it; I could only get so far because I fought with the circumstances in front of me. These circumstances were not what I envisioned for my life and were only temporary, but I would continue to lose focus. I came to believe I wasn't holding fast to my visions with faith. You can judge yourself to the point of feeling unworthy of receiving what you vision.

Your vision is too small. What do I mean? Many of us will realize we must be positive. For instance, you may want to live in a certain neighborhood, but you say to yourself, "I can't afford it." By saying "I can't afford it" voided the vision. Moses was speaking to a burning bush, and he received instructions from God. Moses asked God, "who should I say sent me." God said, "Tell them I am." Here's that word, I am. God created us in his likeness so when God says I am we say I am. If you say I am stupid, I am dumb, I am broke, and they are all negative, then that is what you become. Remember you are a creator. "I am" is how I identify myself. Who am I? "I am" is what I see; which is good. Not what I see which is bad. Your circumstance may look bad, but it will turn around if you start to see a much better you. Let's go back to the house you found in a pricey neighborhood. Why not say I desire this house and I am buying this house. Don't look at the price or your current circumstance. Let your desire line up with the God-conscious or the subconscious mind in you. Let your subconscious mind see only the good things. Remember the conscious mind will reason with your positive and negative. Have you ever heard the cliché; come to a conscious decision? Once you come to a final decision, this is what vibrates to your subconscious mind. The mental picture is what you are painting on the screen of space. This vibe and energy create your path. Make the final decision be a positive one. I have spoken with many people who struggle with vivid mental images or taking a picture and placing themselves in the picture. The conscious mind says you are not there, look around you and see the reality. No matter what the problems or circumstances are, they can be a very temporary thing if you can align yourself with positive thoughts and dreams. The reason some criminals stay in jail is jail is the only vision in the subconscious mind. Their conscious mind can't erase the vision of a jail cell; therefore, they repeat the displayed visual which occupies the field of space. The repetitive visual coupled with the fear of unemployment and lack of productivity plague the mind. I have met guys who say, "I was better off in jail, at least I had food and a bed." Because of my felony record of habitually driving without a driver's license, others assumed I would never get a good job. I ignored it, and have had several good high paying jobs. One reason is I would not limit myself and my ability to have a better life than what I was living. I had to see beyond man's negativity.

The bottom line is to dream big and not limit your dreams based on age, sex, financial status or education. If you can dream it, God, who dwells in you can advance it. Remember as much as you may or may not believe there is a God, I'm here to tell you there is. God created us all, and he created us in his likeness with unconditional love. You will have the God powers of belief whether you are a believer or not, but please understand without acknowledging God or praying (positive meditation and affirmation), the only yielding result is struggling. Many successful people today still believe everything they have came through hard work. Yes, I agree that any success comes first from a thought or vision but leaning towards your own understanding creates hard work. In turn it doesn't seem as rewarding as allowing the God who dwells in us and the holy spirit who we can call on at any time to take us directly to our destiny. Our trust in God and his ways get us where we need to be. Most of the time people who have paved their own way tend to lose what they have obtained because their flesh or ego dictate their direction in life. When we stress we tend not to think clearly, we become frustrated, and everything goes downhill from there.

The best thing for anyone is to surround yourself with people who think big for themselves and think even bigger for you. Someone who sees you bigger than your current situation and gets excited about what they see. This energy is fuel to the universe. When you have several people on the same plane of faith, God's promise is you will always have positive results. You may have something which touched your heart, but you don't know when or where to start. Here is a guide to help you avoid feeling overwhelmed.

1. Write down your vision. Read it or recite it every night before you go to bed.

2. Meditate 15 minutes before you go to bed or early in the morning like 2 or 3 am. I suggest these times because it is a quiet time for meditation.

3. Be careful with who you share this vision. Many people tend to look at current circumstance or even your ability to accomplish what has been placed in your heart.

4. Live in the now as though your vision is already here. Do things you would be doing that is part of your vision. This act is an act of faith.

5. Be patient with God as not to look to see when something is going to happen. Trust your season will come and you will have a full manifestation.

Now, as I spoke in past chapters, you must have patience as well as faith. People ask me why when Jesus was approached by a person for healing, it happened right then. Well, Jesus whom again was sent by God to act as God did as a creator. The reason Jesus would say, "your faith has healed you" is the healings were already done long before the person got to Jesus. Jesus had not yet died which was why it seemed healing was outside of their capability. Their faith in the outer God is the same as the faith in the inner God. The inner God is the promise Jesus made when he said in John 19:13-20 "I will come to you. Before long, the world will not see me anymore, but you will see me. Because I live, you also will live. On that day, you will realize I am in my Father, and you are in me, and I am in you." The inner God will allow you to not only see beyond your basic sight, but you will imagine things you thought you would never imagine. This is what we call God-consciousness. God put something in us before we were conceived in this world. Because of the many distractions in the world, we struggle to find out life's purpose God has for us. There have been people who have attended school for most of their life, and much to their achievement such as obtaining several degrees and even landing the job of their dreams gave it all up because of a greater desire. Understand your passion is not driven by money or any other worldly possession. Love drives this passion deep down inside your soul. Your passion partnered with prayer will present a vivid path which will bring success in everything you do. You will prosper because this is God's law. You will come to know your passion has influenced your subconscious mind so even when you haven't physically walked into it, you will not know the difference. The subconscious mind doesn't understand virtual or reality. Only what you have come to believe. Remember this works for both good and bad.

Let me give you an example of how strongly a person's belief in not doing the right thing will bring about temporary success. I watch this television program called "American Greed." The show features people who have succeeded in life by swindling other people of sometimes their life savings. These people put their trust in the man or women giving a significant portion or all their savings so they can have a retirement fund. This criminal thinks he is doing right by taking their money and even though he has no intention of making them a return on their investment, continues to spend their money to provide for himself a lavish wealthy lifestyle. Now if you ask me, this is the subconscious mind working to attract the wealth he or she envisioned, but this vision was never done by faith in God but by faith in his own ways of obtaining this wealth. Like I have said before, God created us all in his likeness. It doesn't matter if a person is considered bad or good, everyone is created in God's likeness. But because the subconscious mind operates in freewill, it does enable us to do badly as well as doing good. You may ask if he knows they are doing wrong? I can say at first yes, but if a person's conscious mind is convinced they are deserving of this wealthy life then it will happen. It will transfer these thoughts to the subconscious mind. Most of the time I wonder how do they attract these people who are willing to give their money. Sometimes people say, "I am careful with my money because I don't want to give my money to a swindler." However, the very thing they say they don't want is the very thing they attract.

If you have a trust in God, then you will understand God will be your retirement plan. He will send the correct people on your path, and if you should cross one of these swindlers like on this show, you will have a discernment and the God in you will show you that person for whom they really are. This is again the universe working in your favor. It seems all the swindlers and criminals on this show swear they didn't do anything wrong. If you see this, you will find yourself getting angry that this person has just taken someone's life savings. But to be honest, he or she can't take what wasn't theirs. When God establishes wealth in your life, then no one can take it away. This criminal represents the negative intention created by his victim's negative thought. This is law. So, understand as you proceed to think big and as you continue to align yourself with God, your intuition will be enlightened and you will not be convinced of things that don't line up with the power of God. The Holy Spirit will speak in your subconscious before this person arrives. You will not be like Eve who wasn't familiar with the evil thoughts which told her something that didn't align with God. The holy spirit which is God spirit will guide you through all truths.

As this chapter concludes, I want to make sure you understand you are bigger than what you can imagine. Even if you read this book and feel you have it all, there could be something else in your spirit to do, and you look to achieve. A man's outer stature does not also speak of a man's heart. A man can be very wealthy but if you find him to be humble and if you think he has all he needs to accomplish something even greater than himself, then he is grounded in his belief in God. This man doesn't think he has so many riches that he doesn't have to consult infinite intelligence. He knows God is all knowing and the money is something which doesn't concern God. The money will one-day decay or dissolve back into this earth, just as our body. God is spirit as we are spirit. One day we will all reunite with God in this universe. Our heart desires God will provide to us if we ask because He loves us. He is not here to judge our wants. Jesus said in 1 John 2:15-17, "Do not love the world or anything in the world. If anyone loves the world, love for the Father is not in them. For everything in the world—the lust of the flesh, the lust of the eyes, and the pride of life—comes not from the Father but from the world. The world and its desires pass away, but whoever does the will of God lives forever. This man I speak of rich or poor will always desire the love for others as the love God has for him."

Chapter 6

THE SOUL

"For what shall it profit a man, if he gains the whole world and suffers the loss of his soul, Mark 8:36." The referenced scripture explains through the subconscious mind a man can profit the things he believes in which will bring only worldly pleasures. These things are done by his own doings and not by the guidance of the holy spirit which means his soul is not connected to God. He can expect everything he has done that has brought him so called pleasure on earth has forfeited his soul to a miserable life soon to come. The Soul has been a topic of much discussion and argument among many religions. No one has determined if man has a soul or what a soul is yet in the Bible we see the word soul is used by many. Now in the Bible, the word soul wasn't mentioned by God as he created man and woman. Theologians question if the soul was given to man once he became a living being yet Christians have come to the idea their soul will be judged. In Psalms 23:3 the prayer reads "He restores my soul." Psalm 119:20 reads "My soul is consumed with longing for your laws at all time." After my studies of the scriptures, the holy spirit gave me an interpretation. The Soul is where a person's choice is in what God he will serve. As the subconscious mind puts a person's thoughts or beliefs in action on earth, the outcome will determine if this person is trusting in the

Almighty God, the one true God or if he does not have a thought of God or mankind but only himself.

A man's soul obtains redemption through forgiveness which means God restored his soul, but again he must repent of his selfish thinking and be willing to be born again. Born again doesn't mean you will have to die, at least, not a physical death but die a mental death. John 3: 1-21, a man named Nicodemus came to Jesus to confess that he knows Jesus is a teacher from God and no one could do the miracles Jesus performed unless they were with God. Jesus answered, "Most assuredly, I say to you, unless one is born again, he cannot see the kingdom of God." As you continue to read the suggested scriptures in John, you will see Jesus is explaining to him that without Jesus a man is condemned or has condemned himself. God's thinking will always be love and peace for all. No selfish motives. His thoughts are consumed with longing for the laws of God and has made a conscious decision to follow Him.

As we continue to understand the soul, many people have come to believe animals may have a soul. How can this be? An animal doesn't have freewill. God gave created man dominion over all creatures. In Matthew 6:26 Jesus said "Look at the birds of the air, for they neither sow nor reap nor gather into barns; yet your heavenly Father feeds them. Are you not of more value than them? Which of you by worrying can add one cubit to his stature". Man has choices since the fall of the man Adam when God established man will know good from bad. For man has a choice to trust God and his ways or trust his own ways to lead him to destruction. Animals were created to survive by the land as God instructed since creation, therefore it doesn't need a soul because he only knows the one who created him. An animal sees God every day for God is the wind and God's creation is all around them. It is said animals can see spirits. I believe this to be true as I notice my dog staring at certain locations in my house. God too has shown me angels placed in my house in the same location. In John, Jesus was speaking about when you are born of the spirit you will see spiritual things. You will perform miracle acts, but these acts won't seem like a miracle or supernatural because you will feel everything you do is expected. All done because of faith.

When you desire a successful, happy life for you and your family, you must first do some soul searching. I remember in my office on my last job a calm voice said to me "Farris, look at your soul." I thought on this for many days, and I finally told my wife I needed to get my soul right." Now as much as I am familiar with the soul, the thought never crossed my mind that my soul was out of alignment with God. But I admit each day as I looked in the mirror, it was revealed deep within negative thoughts that carried anger, vindictiveness and not a full trust in God. Many people say they believe in God but choose not to trust He will take care of you. This means you don't trust God. To know God is to accept any fate that happens here on earth such as losing a job or not having a job. "Infinite wisdom" will provide for you in ways you wouldn't believe. I struggled with working for someone else as I knew God had more for me. But because I had a family and did not want to fail them, I enslaved myself. My subconscious mind was telling me I would fail them.

Once I found peace, I could let God guide me. I must mention the voice of the Holy Spirit also instructed me to "enter into God's rest." The voice was calm, not demanding or forcing me to change but allowing me to feel free once I agreed. As discussed in the previous chapter, "to enter into Gods rest" is to enter the kingdom of God. Even though the subconscious mind is free will and doesn't know good or bad, I know God is only good, pure and holy. I accept God loves me enough. His spirit heard my cry for a better life and my desire to accept my purpose in life. Finding your purpose brings true happiness. I feel if you can't be happy for you, it will be difficult to be happy for anyone else. There have been instances where parents became jealous or envious of their child's accomplishments because the child chose to go after something that was in the parent's heart. Parents take note, you are never too old even if you feel for whatever reason your accomplishments have been delayed. You are never too late. Remember, God of the universe is timeless. In the Bible, Sara was beyond child bearing years, yet she gave birth. God knew you before you were born and prepared a day when you would accept his calling. When a person enters the kingdom, he or she becomes at peace. Therefore, he or she looks different, acts differently. His or her faith in God and the God within will radiate or like many people will say have a glow on him or her. They will claim, I am healthy, I am wealthy. This person will live in the (I am) state of consciousness. I mentioned before "I am" is man's identity through God. We are God's, so we too are "I am." "I am" is to proclaim with faith our identity with the universe. (I am) follows us without any conscious such as our organs in our body function without any conscious. The energy you speak behind (I am) will reveal the state or position of a person's soul. He or she can say "I am sick, I am broke, I am terrible," and what they speak creates the negative in you, just as speaking all the positives. When you view the negatives, your soul becomes entangled into all works of the flesh. As you repent, take the positive steps and change your thinking.

1. Greet yourself with a cheerful, "good morning" when you arise each day. Don't expect coffee or any other substance to wake you up for in this you dismiss God who wakes you up in the morning.

2. Declare, "Today is a glorious day. God, what can I do today to be a blessing?" Blessing someone exemplifies you are not just making life be about you. You are telling God (the universe) you know you are blessed just to be able to be a blessing. You are also sowing good seeds in your life.

3. Throughout the day, practice thinking positive. If you have been negative most of your life, shifting to daily positives may be difficult. When you get it into your subconscious that thinking positive and treating others like yourself, you will experience happiness throughout the day.

4. Before you go to bed, take the time to meditate on the good things you've done that day. Give thanks to God for such an awesome day. Start speaking the things envisioned and watch how those things manifest. You will find the Holy Spirit revealing things to you with compassion about others.

3 John 1:2 NASB reads, "Beloved, I pray that in all respects you may prosper and be in good health, just as your soul prospers." The apostle John understood a person can be prosperous on earth but his or her soul can be at unrest. When a person prospers without worrying and if he or she loses his or her earthly possession, this will not be a threat to theirs. They know it is God within (the subconscious mind) and all the positive thoughts of "I am" will restore whatever

has been lost. In other words, he or she never lost anything, and he or she never missed it. This person's soul is at peace. When you encounter wealthy people, who may have lost everything to a bad investment, or maybe gambling; it is probably someone who put their trust in earthly treasure. The earthly treasure may have provided a healthy return, but when the person's soul evaluation occurs, the truth is they never gave or helped anyone else without expecting a return. This person probably took the expression "He is God" literally, and not acknowledging the King of Glory. They carry the arrogance of a god who feels the world is theirs. The Bible refers to this as mocking God. Galatians 6:7 reads "Be not deceived; God is not mocked: for whatsoever a man sow, that shall he also reap." A man who boasts is not of the true God. This man is sowing seeds of corruption and when his season comes to reap, it will be of corruption. It is important to stay focused on God, the blesser and not the blessing. The desire of your heart is truly something God promises. I am not saying you shouldn't feel happy you have a beautiful new home or nice cars and jewelry. As I mentioned before, God does not see these things for they are not spirit. These things are created thoughts.

I'm not sure if you have ever heard this prayer, but it is written:

Now I lay me down to sleep;

I pray thee, Lord, my soul to keep,
If I should die before I wake,
I pray thee, Lord, my soul to take.

The author penned this prayer in 1784 in a book catered to children. Now for everything in the book to rhyme seemed to propose the writer didn't understand the meaning of soul yet the intention was good. Let's look at this prayer as this prayer has been passed down for many years. Even today people will have their child recite this because a parent wants their child to have some sense of God in their life. Again, this is good but as a child grows to become an adult and have his or her own family, they will pass along this prayer which is a simple rhyme.

If we look at asking the Lord to keep my soul, does this make any sense? If your soul is based upon the action of choosing God to govern your life or not choosing God, then what is there to keep? God doesn't need to keep your soul- nor does God need to take your soul. Your soul is not something that is a part of you like a kidney, liver or another body part. I have been asked if the soul is connected to the heart. Your heart is your heart. It is something God created in you which allows blood and oxygen from your lungs to travel to all your organs. Your heart is your heart, and your soul is your soul. Don't teach your children your soul is separate from them but teach them their soul measures their choices in life. In the 23rd Psalms, the psalmist says, "He leaded me to still waters; He restores my soul." The still waters are considered a place in our mind of peace. A place where you can reflect on your life. Remember earlier in this chapter I said you should do soul searching. To know God loves you enough to wait for you with open arms is to experience peace with him.

Knowing at the still waters you can change or renew your mind from stress, doubt and worry to a mind directed to God. Isaiah 23:3 reads, "You will keep him in perfect peace, whose mind is stayed on You because he trusts in You." Isaiah when speaking to God knew the love of God would do this for everyone who believes and trusts in God.

To sum up this chapter, I hope you can see your choice to trust God starts by having pure and positive thoughts. Before you make any choice, take the time to ask God for the best path or decision for you and your family. If you have faith, God will always give you an answer and place in your subconscious mind the correct path you will need to take. You will understand your soul is aligned with God.

Chapter 7

Friends

As you read this book, you may wonder what do friends have to do with creating a successful life for your family? We will break down the word "friend" and the influence your friend or friends may have on your life. When I was younger, I would always hear stories from my peers about how their girlfriend's friend would always seem to have a comment about their relationship. I could only assume the friend was envious so the friend would give advice from a negative perspective. Therefore, she would not provide the best advice. All friends are not envious of your success, or that you are dating this hot guy or this gorgeous woman. However, if you are not present in the spirit of God, which gives you the power of discernment then you probably would be far from noticing if their spirit is truth or not. In 1 Corinthians 15:33 reads "Do not be misled: Bad company corrupts good character." I find this to be very true. Look at your friends and analyze your friendship. When you need them, will their character appear to be sketchy? You may notice if when you need them, will they still be that friend? You will see how this is important as they can be an influence on your life and to your relationship. Sometimes a spouse; for some reason, will pick up on her husband's friend whose habits are a bad influence on your husband. Many marriages have come to the point of separation or worst a divorce because of friends. Genesis 2:24 reads "For this reason a man shall leave his father and his mother, and be joined to his wife, and they shall become one flesh." Understand, you and your wife are united in spirit. Therefore, if your relationship is at odds because you have been friends with someone since you were in college or before marriage; It's time to make the necessary separation. The length of the friendship is invalid when it comes to your marriage. Just as a man will leave his mother and father, he should be willing to move away from whatever is in his past such as old memories of how you and your friends partied and lived life without a care.

Emotions play an important part in our life when it comes to departing with friends. After all, these are the friends that were part of your wedding. Because of our history or connection, we find some obligation to keep them around. Why? A true friend will be happy your life is moving forward. I agree it's okay to converse from time to time. However, if you are married and your friend isn't, then his or her input or advice puts you on two different playing fields. For example, you and your friend decide to go to a bar for a night out on the town. Your friend is strictly there to grab a mate. And while you are there your friend meets someone who has a friend. This friend may be married as well, but just as you are supporting your friend, they are doing the same. Now the notion of temptation is open because the person with him or her is very attractive and may be attracted to you. I am not saying you may fall for them but why put yourself in the situation. I feel once you get closer to your husband or wife, the more you will pull away from this friend.

What if you both are married and as friends, you go out for drinks or a night on the town? I find no problem with this if you both understand enjoying your night and not falling into your friend's sob story that their marriage has been on the rocks for years and this is the best time they have had in years. Before you know it, you are convinced you should not have to put up with the negatives about your spouse. Temptation presents the idea that you and your spouse never do any fun things so now you don't feel guilty for enjoying yourself with this friend. These influences are the very thing that can create negative vibrations. God is God, and God is in you. The best way to come to an answer about your relationship with friends is to go before God in meditation. As you relax and breathe deeply, you will sense a spirit of peace which is the Holy Spirit. You will receive all answers, but the beauty of the spirit of God is this spirit doesn't cause you to react negatively. God is not the author of confusion, 1 Corinthians 14:33. You will find your friend will gracefully move away or become so occupied that you won't spend as much time as you once did. What God wants is the best for you and your friend. Through your peace, you can now visualize your friend's happiness and their marriage becoming better. The friend who is single, visualize he or she finds the person of their dream. In 1545 William Turner wrote a version of this expression in a paper "Byrdes of one Kynde and color flok and flye allwayes together." The way we hear it is, "birds of a feather will flock together."

You can come to your own conclusion if you and your friend/friends have the same spirit and attitude. As I mentioned earlier, if you are happily married would your friend act as though he or she is happily married? If for some reason your friend's perspective of marriage is interpreted as bondage, boring, or the feeling of never again having fun; then a happy marriage is far from their thoughts. My wife and

I are always doing things, and we enjoy each other's company. I don't have a vast number of friends. It's ok if you and your spouse are the same. My wife is my friend as well as my companion. This is how you should view your spouse. You know no one will have your best interest as much as the one to whom you are connected. It is fine if you don't seem to have friends in your life now. When the time comes, you will attract the right friends but only if you put this in your subconscious.

I want to paint a picture of how our subconscious forms images. I tell my kids all the time everything we imagine starts as a seed. At some point, the seed becomes full grown. For example, you go out with your single friend, and you have a wonderful time. You and your friend meet these two women/men and the night is a blast. Let's look at the scenario we have here. You remove your wedding ring at your friend's request. The state of consciousness negotiates good or bad, right or wrong. Removing your ring could be harmless, but now the subconscious starts to paint the single picture. The energy you are sending is you are single. Why? Maybe you are enjoying the company of a different person other than your spouse. Matter of fact they are the total opposite of your spouse. You start to attract the energy your friend is reflecting, and when the friend suggests you go out again, you accept. Your mind will facilitate different stories to tell your spouse. You are sure your spouse won't believe any of the lies so you create ways you can hang out again. Now you are not doing it for your friend but yourself. Your seed is taking sprout. Months later this little meeting you have with this person has turned into an affair, a full-grown seed. We as humans are weak in the flesh, and we should indulge in continuous meditation and prayer to make sure we are directed on the right path. Once your thoughts turn to a negative path, your soul begins to harvest negative fruit. You will start to find things that once worked for you no longer work. For example, on your job, you could be the top salesman but lately, your sales are falling, and you find yourself late for work because your spirit is not at rest. In the last chapter, I spoke of entering the kingdom of God. Once a man falls out of the kingdom, it means he has limited his access to the benefits of the all-knowing God. He doesn't have the discernment he once had. He starts to blame everything happening on his wife rather than taking ownership of his own demise. Take note that this example applies to men or women. Thinking wrong is not gender specific. Every action we take in our life will have a consequence. This is the law of sowing and reaping. As mentioned in an earlier chapter, if you have children, this will affect the energy in your household. The man is the head of the household and the royal priest of your house. It doesn't matter if you make less money or not. God established this headship with Adam. But when a man falls out of grace with God, he can corrupt his household. If your wife is a praying woman, she will be there to pray God's grace upon your marriage simply because the vows she accepted were to be there for each other through thick and thin. From this point, you have the choice to maintain your marriage or go after a vision not of God.

In 2 Samuel 11, King David sent Joab and his servants out to war. One evening David arose from his bed and walked on the roof of the king's house in which he saw this beautiful woman bathing. David learned the woman's name was

Bathsheba, and she was married. David didn't care much about the fact she was married. He called for Bathsheba, and he laid with her. Later she bore a child by David. Now Bathsheba's husband was a devoted servant to David. To cover his mess, David got him drunk and had him to go to the frontlines of the battle to fight. From there he was killed. The consequences of David's actions were he could not win in battle and the son Bathsheba bore became ill and died.

When our thoughts are of selfishness which lacks love, and we do things without love, things don't end well. God is not the author of confusion. Good can't come out of a confusing situation. Not just in ways we would desire. Depending on where we are in life, we should take the wrong we have done and learn from it. If you feel you and your spouse are to move on then be patient and let God direct your life and release your spouse. It was God who allowed Moses to give a certificate of divorce because he knew man is stubborn. For God says when you lay with a woman, you have taken her as your bride. Thank God for his risen Son who died on the cross, so we won't get punished for breaking God's law given to his people during the time of Moses. The married man who thinks he has met someone better than his wife will soon see he has fallen for the lust of the flesh. This means he fell for the very thing Christ was tempted by in the wilderness and Eve was tempted by the serpent in the garden. God does not tempt, but your temptation is by your own subconscious mind. Jesus spoke, "Be in this world but not as this world." Being in this world means driven by beauty and sex, pride and boastfulness. You can have a life in heaven created in your subconscious mind, and you can enjoy a wonderful life, but as the Christ in you is risen, you as the Christ won't be tempted by these things. You will not shift your focus from the grace God has upon you, like David.

Now that you have read this chapter, ask yourself, what is a friend? I found a good online definition of a friend: a person who gives assistance, a patron or supporter. All the attributes are positive as in the meaning it has the verb 'give.' A friend should never put you or your family in a tempting situation. A friend will only give the positive but will never say "If I was you." I've never cared for this terminology because we are individuals. I am not anyone, but I am one with God. If you and your friend are like minded as you and you know the right thing to do in your life, then you and your friend will come in agreement. Matthew 18:20 reads "For where two or three are gathered in my name, there am I among them." Because each of us has God in us and if we both are aligned with God this means I won't have to be you. The scripture shows I am one with you in the universe. God is universe. The universe is spirit. This is the only way we are connected and not by the flesh.

My kids use the word "friend" very loosely as all kids do. It's funny because they can be friends for a month or so but when I ask what happened to the friend they were hanging out with, they will say "we don't hang out anymore." I ask them all the time, how they come to call this person a friend? Their answer is usually, "because we talk." "Wow," I would say. My thought was if that was me I would say I have many friends because I talk to many people. But now I look at Facebook. Facebook has "friend request" where people have up to 3,000 "friends" yet probably actually knows only 1/5 of them. People are hurt when it comes to friends because maybe they haven't been taught the true definition of friend.

I will never let the world system dictate my friendship. I like to think of a friend as a person who won't tell me what I want to hear but what I need to hear. A friend will not infringe on your life and will always bring Godly advice and not advise from their emotions. Even in the event of a disagreement, a friend will not hold a grudge for days or months. They will not rest until the disagreement is resolved. As friends, both of you should feel this way. You won't let the sun go down until you deal with the issue. That is why I say if you are married the best friend is your spouse. This is whom you have grounded your relationship and friendship with. Never let that friendship go. This is the one-person God has given so appreciate him or her.

Never create a friend out of desperation. Never feel alone and say I don't have a friend or friends. This mindset causes you to allow anyone into your life without discerning their character. You should first create a friend in your mind. Speak to the friend every day and imagine the friend sitting with you in the morning drinking coffee or tea or in the evening conversing about life. You will attract that type of friend. Never feel you are pathetic or lonely because you desire to have the perfect person as a friend in your life. Finding a friend is the same as finding a mate. This is a person who is in your life for a reason, whether they are there for a season or if they are there for a lifetime.

Chapter 8

Who Am I?

Have you ever taken a close look at yourself in the mirror and asked yourself who am I? What do you think of yourself? If you are a mother do you say, "I am a mother" or same for a father, do you say, "I am a father" or do you say, "I am a husband" or "I am a wife." Because the words (I am) is so important to your spirit, to what do you say, "I am?" You may see books or audio of many authors who speak of "I am." In Exodus 3:1-15 Moses was speaking to a burning bush which was God. God had commanded he speak to the Israelites concerning their captivity by the Egyptian. He was preparing the Elders and leaders to speak to Pharaoh. Moses asked God who shall I say sent me. God said, "tell them I Am sent you." "I am" is a powerful statement. When you are in the "I am" state of mind that is what you become.

Now this "I Am" state of mind is just like the subconscious mind. It doesn't discriminate. I Am doesn't know good or bad. Why? Because we are created in God's image and the image of God allows us to create. "I am good, I am bad, I am happy, I am sick, I am poor, I am wealthy" and so on, gets into the subconscious mind and what the subconscious mind projects thus far is what you become.

Let's first look at the word "I." The word I doesn't reference anyone else but only the individual. When saying the word "I" you are taking on the responsibility of whatever tag you place on yourself is not shared with anyone else. Each "I" takes on its own identity. So, when you say, "I am rich" No one else shares your identity. It doesn't mean you are selfish in your thought; it just means I am. Oneness. "Am" is a word that only follows the word "I" in the English language. I am, is what defines us as humans. When you say the words "I am" means what other word or words which follow is rooted in the field of space. Whatever I am is what I have chosen to be. No matter if I meant it or not. It has been planted in the subconscious mind. When God told Moses "I am who I am," it proved to me to be a powerful statement because God is stating the universe can't be anything else. Because God is all infinite, all knowing, all omniscient and so on means there is no lack or falling short of anything. Can you imagine if you could only see the greatest in your potential?

Do you ever wonder why do we fall short of our potential to be the greatest father or mother or husband or wife? An excellent question. To answer this question, we must look at our emotions. Our emotions as I mentioned before dictates our "I am." When we get into an argument, we tend to feel sad. So now you're "I am" is I am sad. You may say "I am human" and this is the very reason. Remember when I mentioned in the earlier chapters we are spirit beings? When you were created by God in spirit, the only emotions you carry are love, peace, and happiness. To see the good in everything for your benefit is what God shows us as Jesus walked the earth. But there were times when Jesus' displayed his human side. For example, when he cried in the garden of Gethsemane and when He was in God's temple when people were there selling animals rather than using the temple for worship. He was furious as he cleared out the temple. As I look at these emotions, I see we are allowed emotions as humans, but it's how we react with these emotions that make the difference. Sometimes people become very vindictive in their emotions thus they start to paint this picture in the subconscious mind of something evil. And on the other hand, a person is happy and will want to do something special for someone, so they paint this picture of buying a gift or celebrating. The two examples I gave was a prime example of "I am." Would it be safe to say Jesus would have said "I am angry" when he was in the temple or "I am sad" when he wept in the garden of Gethsemane? I would say yes. So, as you say, " I am human," how far does a person go with that expression? Is it an excuse to behave in a particular manner whether good or bad? A happy expression should be the only thing we should know since we are spirit. We should live by the spirit, be governed by the spirit and blessed in the spirit. Every emotion outside of happy should be a temporary emotion. When we choose to let fleshly thoughts and emotion become involved to the point it stays with us for a while, we slowly reject the spirit of God in us. So, this leads me back to the question, who are you? When you are angry with your child(ren), is it because you are human(flesh)? Or do you tend to practice the Agape love of forgiveness and understanding (spirit)? Now in this book, we have established God is everything and God knows everything. After scolding your child(ren), do you still feel like a good parent? Sometimes we do question ourselves as we love our child (ren) so much, and we only want the best for them, but we force thoughts and beliefs on them they aren't capable of understanding. If you look at how you are forcing your understanding of life on your child and punishing him or her by labeling him or her as stubborn, you may begin to question your methods. Through this behavior, your subconscious mind only views your child(ren) in one light, and that is stubborn. Yes, we say it all the time, he or she is stubborn. And we all as parents tend to say he or she is "just like your father or mother." We should know why our child(ren) will rebel. When you start to question the "I am" in you means you are losing your identity as a parent in this case. This actually goes for husband or wife." I remember growing up when there were times my grandmother just stopped fussing at me, and she would sit in her rocking chair and say nothing. Now I am not saying she wouldn't talk, but when I wasn't behaving in the manner she knew I should, she wouldn't speak on it. She would just give me a hug and say, "I love my grandson." Later I realized she prayed and visualized a better outcome for me and by doing it this way means she was connected to God in spirit. She wasn't going to prove to the world what type of parent she was by enforcing actions and words the world thinks a parent should do or say. I admit I have been guilty of this until I came to an understanding that when I put my kids in God's hands to help me to raise them means I must trust infinite intelligence will guide me through the holy spirit. I only look for good outcomes, no matter what is seen. Again, your vision is the now and if you see a good outcome in your meditation/prayer means the present state will change.

So "I Am" is connected to your soul simply because you can choose to think you are something great. But if what you claim to be with your actions brings not joy but worry, stress to everyone else and you tend to get pleasure from others misery means, then your soul is not aligned with God, and at some point, all you have put out will come back to you.

Remember "I Am" doesn't know good or bad. So again, ask yourself "who am I"? What is your life's purpose for your child(ren) or your spouse? When you married, your spouse did you not understand you became one in spirit. So, when you are intimate, you are worshipping God, and the Bible says he that worships God must worship in spirit and in truth. Again, ask yourself "who am I?" To be intimate is to love. God is love. People use the word love and intimate very loosely as it has no meaning anymore. But God's love is pure and intimate, and since we are the creation of God in his image, we should have the same love, the same intimate feelings which are pure in our worshipping. When you are making love to your wife or husband, realize what you are. A creator (I am a creator), you are love (I am love), you are spirit (I am spirit), you are peace (I am peace), you are patient (I am patient), you are trustworthy (I am trustworthy). Measure yourself to these things as you meditate. Recite them at night before you go to bed. You will start to realize as spirit you are everything God called you to be. Never look at what you have done or what you were labeled based on those things you have done and are ashamed. But now you are reborn. You have repented from old thoughts. Learn to forgive yourself as God has already forgiven you. The world speaks of forgiveness but doesn't know forgiveness. Forgiveness is love, and love forgets those things of old. Think about a person who lives in a small town where everybody knows everybody. This person was known for something bad in which the town wouldn't let them forget. This person grows up and leaves town, never to return. This person starts his or her life over with a family, a successful and happy life. This is what happens when you repent from negative thoughts that dictate your "I am." When you seek God, you change your thinking, and you change all of what is in your subconscious mind. The reason a person can't forget the things of old is they are bound by words in the subconscious mind. Remember this is the mind of God. God wants you to be happy. Romans 12:2, "And do not be conformed to this world, but be transformed by the renewing of your mind, that you may prove what is that good and acceptable and perfect will of God." Understand everything is in the mind. By renewing your mind is to make new again. At some point, our subconscious mind has been developed since we were about six years old and we have continued to collect worldly thoughts that have held us in bondage. You deserve the perfect life, and the only way to do that is to realize who you are.

Have you ever watched a movie where the villain, normally the head of some organization no one can touch says, "Do you know who I am"? As you watch the way the character emphasizes that phrase, he may show emotion and strength as he is speaking because he knows what power he possesses. Now if he didn't have money, bodyguards, and probably government officials on his side, the phrase wouldn't mean much. There are people today in those situations who feel this very way. We know God is much more powerful than these people, but Christians don't seem to take hold of this power of "I am" God has in us. Now remember "I Am" is power and people will take it to a dark side, but God is light so your "I Am" should always be a positive affirmation. When using "I am" with a depressed or negative connotation, it produces a continuous destructive life.

Albert Einstein's theory of E=MC² which is the law of relativity discovered in 1905 brought on the theory in the universe is matter. We are part of the universe, and everything around us is matter. Matter is made up of tiny energy (atoms, electrons) thus producing power. His equation opened the door of further studies which showed the electromagnetic field produced by a cell reflects the frequency of its vibration. The law of vibration (in which this theory was called) simply states everything moves and everything vibrates. Scientists have proven our physical, mental, emotional and spiritual vibrations are at different frequencies. Fear and anxiety vibrate at a very low frequency, but love and joy vibrate at a much higher frequency. Our frequency of vibration of God is 512 and 528 Hz. These frequencies are said to be the sound of middle c on a music scale. This is the third note on the scale, and it relates to the note "MI." "MI" comes from the Latin phrase "MI-ra-gestor um" meaning "miracle." Hospitals today practice using different levels of vibration to heal patients. Can you imagine doctors who are usually not big on traditional medicine but modern medicine has come to the need of God? The studies show people sick of diseases were healed when they heard music at different frequencies such as 528 Hz frequency. This is to prove that "I am healing" was present. When we listen to music that puts us in bad or foul moods or moods of destruction when measured was said to be at the frequencies of 741 Hz and 440 Hz better known as the devil's interval. You can do more research on this but my point is to show how God is all around us and there is no getting away from him. Nikola Tesla "If you want to find the secrets of the universe, think regarding energy, frequency, and vibration." Albert Einstein "Everything is energy, and that's all there is to it. Match the frequency of the reality you want, and you cannot help but get that reality. It can be no other way." When you realize the power within you to change every negative thing around you by changing what you hear, you will come to an understanding that you can change so many things in this world. I am not here to say you can change the world, but you can make a difference in your surroundings. As I mentioned before, as you change you will see changes in your spouse, your child(ren) and friends that are not to be a part of your life will suddenly stop coming around. We sometimes feel like if we don't have friends, then we are weird but you are not weird. You want to have people who are on the same wave-length as you. You never want people around with a negative vibration that is going to bring your vibration down. With higher vibrations, you usher in the holy spirit. You feel joyous and vibrant. You won't feel lost or confused. Your mind will be at ease. Take the time to see who you are and know God created you to be all you can be.

Chapter 9

Where do you live?

Have you ever thought to ask yourself, where does your mind or spirit dwell? This may seem to be a trick question, but my intention is to get your thoughts pointed away from your physical body. As I have said throughout this book God is Spirit. God sees everything in the spirit realm. People tend to make statements such as: "my life is a living hell," "that man (or woman) took me through hell," "my job is hell," "I'm in heaven," or "I must be in heaven." Even though we may not think about what we say but I must remind you that you are a creator. Does it mean that being a creator you create your own heaven or hell? As a child, I believed one day I would be judged for the actions on earth and these actions will determine if I will go through the pearly gates of heaven or in the fiery furnace of hell. Now I am not here to challenge anyone's belief but let's look at this from a different angle. Brimstone is an inflammable substance found on the shores of the Dead Sea. When it burns, it creates a suffocating odor. The soil around Sodom and Gomorrah abounded in Sulphur and Bitumen. The men who recorded these figurative events only referenced what were familiar. So maybe as John was writing the book of Revelation, he could only describe the worst situation a person could experience for his or her sins on earth. He knew Brimstone was this terrible mineral that would burn eyes and lungs if a person came in contact. If this body is temporary, then it will not see heaven or hell, because it decays. As I have said before, this book is not a reference to religion. Words can take on different meanings. You must let the Holy Spirit speak to you so you can understand what the author of each book was conveying. Now I tend to think of the expression, "your soul will burn in hell." I already explained in another chapter our soul is tied to how we are thinking and living. Think about a person who is addicted to a drug. Every day this person is relying on a substance to help him or her cope with life not realizing his or her spirit is what's suffering. The body then starts to take the shape of what their spirit is going through. That is why when you see people who are truly addicted to crystal meth, or heroin you may say "he or she looks like hell." They may even tell you they feel like they are going through hell. Now compare it to fire and brimstone. What could be worse? Will this person have to face this fire and brimstone again when they die or are they facing this torment every day through the torture of drugs? God's reference in the Bible is always for us to think from a spiritual point of view. Again, I say a person can live in hell on earth. A corrupt thought can lead to a corrupt life. A corrupt life is what you may start to sow, so you will reap what you have done. This is the law.

We also have those who are reaping the benefits of blessing others. Those whom have put their trust in God and are following the path God laid in their heart. Ask this person how are they living, and they may very well say "My life is like heaven." See heaven doesn't have to be a big house or nice cars. Your heaven may be living on a farm with a simple house or after sacrificing to put your child through school and see them graduate and have a successful life. The child may show their thanks and love by giving you a beautiful house and say you don't have to work another day in your life. God's ways are not your ways so understand trusting in God means you don't know the next step. You only see the outcome. That outcome is what you created. Martin Luther King had a quote I use to measure my faith. He said, "Take the first step in faith. You don't have to see the whole staircase, just take the first step." Can you imagine by trusting in God and placing trust into your subconscious mind, it allows you to have a stress-free life? We assume we want the next step to happen in a certain way at a certain time and if life doesn't present to us the steps in the way we want things to happen, then we start to stress and worry. If you take that first step towards what you desire in faith, accept you may not know how you are going to get it, but if you visualize it, then it is already done.

In Luke 8:41-56, it is the story where Jesus raises Jairus' daughter from the dead. I looked at the girl as a person in a coma. When you are in a coma, it is said you are in a state of unconsciousness. I have read testimonies of people saying they could see themselves and everyone else, as though they left their body. Even individuals who have died have given the same testimonies. Because we are spirit beings, this shows the body can be cold, still and barely functioning but the spirit continues to live. What do we mean when we say a person is unconscious? Does it mean not aware? If so then it can be contradicting to a person who is in a coma. When giving testimonies, people said they were aware of everything being said. I was reading an article about this young lady who was in a coma who said she felt very cold. In her mind she was in Alaska, but she was in the hospital in California with ice packs all around her body. Maybe this is proof of the subconscious mind. Let's take Jairus' daughter, if her father and everyone around had pronounced her dead, then we can ask "what died?" Did her flesh die or did her spirit die? John 3:16 reads "For God so loved the world that he gave his one and only Son, that whoever believes in him shall not perish but have eternal life." Now I would like to break this down once again. God's one and only son is the word of God in flesh.... or you can say the deity of God which is love. Believing in God means trusting in God which means you are entering the kingdom of God. Eternal life is not expressed in the physical body but the spirit. Let's look at the girl in the coma again, can we determine after her death she is aware of what is going on. I have also read stories of people who have died, and I would say it is somewhat the same feeling. These people said they felt very peaceful and they were aware of what was going on but they were in a state of consciousness. One young lady said she thought of being in a place she had never been and just like that; she was there. They all said they saw a bright light and lots of colors. I also read a person had a different reaction, no lights and the voices couldn't be made out. I feel when you are physically unconscious you are spiritually conscious and you can make a choice of what you perceive. I look at how we are spirit, and we are energy. In the last chapter, I talked about the law of vibration. The universe, which is all knowing, all seeing, produces matter. We are matter. Therefore, we are energy. Everything that moves has a vibration. This vibration creates tones and colors. When people die, I feel they are connecting to the oneness of God. Their spirit is moving thus creating a frequency which allows them to see the colors. Many have said they hear this majestic and peaceful music.

I have had out-of-body experiences in my life, and I felt a sense of peace, power, and awareness. I not only saw myself but I could see events such as two guys sitting in their car, or a guy in a depressed state in his home. I later prophesied to the people of what I saw. These people were contemplating suicide, but as I was there, they didn't. I could tell each of these men at different times as I met them they were thinking suicide. The remarkable thing about my occurrences is I never went looking for these people nor had I met them before. This is not science. Because God has such a strong connection to his creation which is us on earth, we can connect to the universe through thought and imagination which means we leave the world of sight. That is why when you meditate or daydream, you are not aware of your earthly place. Just as if you were dead or in a coma. Now let's not get this confused when I say you can see everything or hear people talking. What I mean is even though you are aware, you don't have a second thought of what is happening. When you connect with God, your consciousness stops reasoning. I did read where this man felt disappointed of not accomplishing his goals on earth, and he said he had an infinite sadness while the others I spoke of said they had an infinite happiness. As you see the conscious mind doesn't go back or forth in this state but in a choice, choose whether you are happy or sad is what you become...even when you are dead by the world's standard. Our state of mind is important to our state of being. You don't have to die or go into a coma to view your life. Being in a coma or dying does allow you a moment to reflect on your life. As bad as this may seem everyone needs to allow themselves that moment. But why not get into the practice of evaluating your life mentally through meditation. Imagine your life being free and focus on what you see yourself having, living and being. Close your eyes from what your physical eyes see. Create your own coma if that works for you or hypnotize yourself. Some clinics teach people how to have an- out- of body experience. If these clinics assist in getting you to the point you need to be so your subconscious mind can take a different direction, then I would say go for it.

So now I ask again, where do you live? Maybe so far you don't have a definitive answer, and that's ok. There is a thing of contentment. A person who may be appreciative every day of the life they live even though they haven't reached their full potential but is patient is a person living in contentment. This is only for the individual who trusts in the Almighty God for their daily direction. This person can consider he or she is living in heaven but like I mentioned, aren't quite there yet. But for the person whose life is not fully in hell but feels nothing is going right, may ask what state will be considered for me since I haven't fully bottomed out yet? There isn't a word to define this state, but I will say if you are at a place where you can change your thinking that will put you in a state of contentment, then you should start right away. If your life is a living hell and that is where you see yourself, why would you go to a place where you are already dwelling? One person had infinite happiness, and another had had infinite sadness. Nothing was mentioned of a pit full of fire. Now if the subconscious mind chooses to take them there than there is where he or she will be. One should never think his or her life is so bad to say, "I am miserable" and thus creating hell in his or her life for eternity. You can say it is amazing how strong our mind is. I must admit at times I fight with my conscious mind when it comes to feeling happy or frustrated. I know when I feel frustrated I'm becoming impatient and if I am impatient, I am not trusting God. But when I am happy I can wait patiently until my appointed time for what I have asked. For myself, I choose not to live in a state of frustration creating a life with a lack of trust and love. I can see how this can create a very miserable life and even a life labeled as hell. Again, I pray and meditate at least three times daily. I find time to seek God to keep my self-aligned with him. It is God who created me, and it is God who promises his spirit to guide me. I have come to understand all things are God. So why should I resist a God who has offered me peace from having a life of living hell? If it has become so evident by many who have witnessed the power of "I am" and has become so successful by just applying the law of love into their life, then I don't understand why so many people choose to be bitter or unforgiving. The same people complain they haven't been dealt a fair hand. I hear the expression life isn't fair, but I ask by whose standards? Life is what you create it to be. What would be unfair is if God did not allow you free will. You decide your outcome every day by what you think or speak. So, ask yourself, do you think life is unfair to you? I know we look at the world and we see poverty, sickness among children and so many other things would make you wonder if God is this awesome being. But how many people have helped the impoverished people or the sick children by renewing their thinking? We only hear or see the bad things in the news, but little of the good things are revealed. You belong to God, and you have the power to change what needs to be changed. When a person thinks, he is judging God, he is only judging himself. You become a co-contributor to creating someone else's hell when you spend a day complaining about a situation rather than asking the Holy Spirit to show you how to fix the situation. The bottom line is this: You are everything God has made you to be. You are part of a dynamic universe which is God. You can look beyond your present state knowing as you grow in God, you can achieve all that it is for you on this earth. With knowing that, look forward to making your life on earth heaven.

About the Author

Farris Patterson is a former pastor and motivational coach that has served in ministry for over 20 years. He has coached many individuals and families with the struggles of family and life. He takes the teaching of Jesus' ministry of love from the bible, other religious views of God's love as well as his personal encounters with life as motivation and learning tools.

Farris resides in California with his wife and children.

To learn more about Farris, visit his website at:

www.visionn5d.com

www.ingramcontent.com/pod-product-compliance
Lightning Source LLC
Chambersburg PA
CBHW072104290426
44110CB00014B/1818